WONDERS of the WORLD ATLAS

NEIL MORRIS

World Book

in association with
WCN

Titles available
Animal Atlas
Wonders of the World Atlas

Text: Neil Morris
Consultant: Graham Peacock
Main illustrations: Sebastian Quigley, Gary Bines
Computer illustrations: Mel Pickering, Jacqueline Land
Managing editor: Deborah Kespert
Editor: Julia Hillyard
Editorial support: Robert Sved, Inga Phipps, Amanda Nathan, Flavia Bertolini
Art director: Belinda Webster
Design support: Helen Holmes, Alex Frampton, Gareth Dobson
Picture research: Laura Cartwright
U.S. Editor: Sharon Nowakowski

First published in the United States by
World Book Publishing
525 W. Monroe
Chicago, IL 60661
in association with Two-Can, Ltd.

**For information on other World Book products, call 1-800-255-1750, x2238,
or visit our Web site at http://www.worldbook.com**

Library of Congress Cataloging-in-Publication Data
Morris, Neil, 1946-
    Wonders of the world atlas / Neil Morris.
        p.   cm.
    Includes index.
    Summary: Text, photographs, and maps explore places of natural
    beauty and notable buildings all around the world, including rivers,
    forests, ancient, modern, and religious structures.
    ISBN 0-7166-9600-2 (hardback). — ISBN 0-7166-9601-0 (pbk.)
    1. Children's atlases. [1. Curiosities and wonders.
    2. Atlases.] I. Title.
    G1021 .M76 1998 <G&M>
    912--DC21   98-10046

Hardback   2 3 4 5 6 7 8 9 02 01 00 99 98
Paperback 2 3 4 5 6 7 8 9 02 01 00 99 98

Photographic credits: ABPL/Graeme Williams p34 tr; Ancient Art & Architecture Collection Ltd: p33 tr; B & C Alexander/Ann Hawthorne p9;
Britstock - IFA/Eric Bach p18, Britstock - IFA/Günter Graefenhain p23 tl, Britstock - IFA/Aberham p25 bl; Images: p11 bl, p19 bl, p31 tr, p43 bl;
James Davis Photography: p37 bl; National Geographic/James P Blair p27 tr; Pictor International Ltd: p12 tr, p13 tl, p13 cr, p15 tl, p19 tr, p24, p25 tl;
Sanford & Agliolo/Science Photo Library: p8; Tony Stone Images: TSI/Philip & Karen Smith p10, TSI/Mike Vines p11 tr, TSI/Bob Thomason p12 bl,
TSI/Cosmo Condina p16, TSI/Suzanne Murphy p17 tl, TSI/John Lamb cover, p26, p43 tr, p45 cr, TSI/Geoff Johnson p27 bl, TSI/Nabeel Turner p30,
TSI/John Beatty p32, TSI/Daryl Balfour p34, TSI/Michael Busselle p35, TSI/David Sutherland p36, TSI/Hugh Sitton p37 tl, TSI/Hilarie Kavanagh p40,
TSI/Keren Su p40 tr, TSI/Doug Armand p41 br, TSI p42, TSI/Paul Chesley p44; TRIP/Robert Belbin p17 br, TRIP/Terry Why p22, TRIP/C Rennie p31 br;
The Stock Market/Zaanse Schans p23 br, The Stock Market/Weissgekleideter Einwohner vor Moschee p33 bl.

Printed in Hong Kong

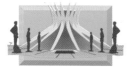

Contents

How to use this book

There are spectacular buildings and natural wonders all over the world. Each map in this book shows you where some are found. Look at the page below to find out how to use the maps. You'll also find a helpful glossary and index at the back of the book.

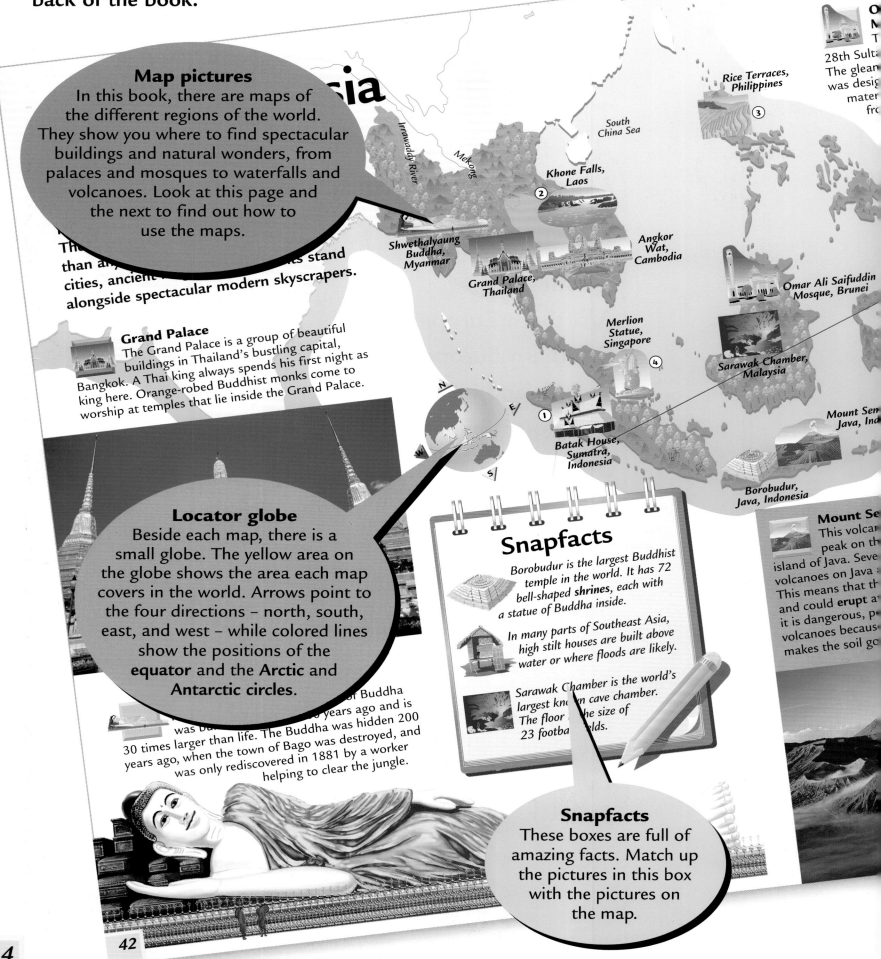

Map pictures
In this book, there are maps of the different regions of the world. They show you where to find spectacular buildings and natural wonders, from palaces and mosques to waterfalls and volcanoes. Look at this page and the next to find out how to use the maps.

Locator globe
Beside each map, there is a small globe. The yellow area on the globe shows the area each map covers in the world. Arrows point to the four directions – north, south, east, and west – while colored lines show the positions of the **equator** and the **Arctic** and **Antarctic** circles.

Grand Palace
The Grand Palace is a group of beautiful buildings in Thailand's bustling capital, Bangkok. A Thai king always spends his first night as king here. Orange-robed Buddhist monks come to worship at temples that lie inside the Grand Palace.

The ... of Buddha was bu... years ago and is 30 times larger than life. The Buddha was hidden 200 years ago, when the town of Bago was destroyed, and was only rediscovered in 1881 by a worker helping to clear the jungle.

Snapfacts

Borobudur is the largest Buddhist temple in the world. It has 72 bell-shaped **shrines**, each with a statue of Buddha inside.

In many parts of Southeast Asia, high stilt houses are built above water or where floods are likely.

Sarawak Chamber is the world's largest known cave chamber. The floor ... the size of 23 footba... elds.

Snapfacts
These boxes are full of amazing facts. Match up the pictures in this box with the pictures on the map.

(Map labels:) Rice Terraces, Philippines; South China Sea; Khone Falls, Laos; Irrawaddy River; Mekong; Shwethalyaung Buddha, Myanmar; Grand Palace, Thailand; Angkor Wat, Cambodia; Omar Ali Saifuddin Mosque, Brunei; Merlion Statue, Singapore; Sarawak Chamber, Malaysia; Batak House, Sumatra, Indonesia; Mount Se... Java, Ind...; Borobudur, Java, Indonesia

Mount Se...
This volcan... peak on th... island of Java. Seve... volcanoes on Java ... This means that th... and could **erupt** a... it is dangerous, p... volcanoes becaus... makes the soil go...

Modern wonders

During the 1900's, new materials and modern technology have brought exciting advances in building design. Many cities are packed with towering skyscrapers and museums in unusual shapes. All of these places are built for the way we live today and for how we plan to spend our time in the future.

Atomium
This unusual Belgian monument was built in 1958. It is made up of nine hollow balls, linked together by long metal tubes.

Chrysler Building
The Chrysler Building was completed in 1930. It stands in New York, a city famous for its skyscrapers.

Worker and the Collective Farm Girl.
This imposing steel statue was put up for an exhibition in Russia, in the 1940's.

Guggenheim Museum
The Guggenheim Museum, in New York City, is made entirely out of concrete. Its smooth sides curve out and up, like a spring.

Pompidou Center
The unique design of the Pompidou Center, in France, shocked many people when it was built in the 1970's.

Petronas Towers
When these two 88-story office buildings in Malaysia were completed in 1996, they became the tallest in the world.

The Chrysler Building is an office built for a well-known car manufacturer. The gleaming metal circles at the top of the building were designed to look like giant car wheels.

The figures of the Worker and the Farm Girl carry a hammer and sickle in their hands. These tools of industry and farming are a symbol for how people can achieve more by working together.

Inside the Guggenheim Museum, a long spiral walkway curves all the way up to the roof. Hundreds of visitors pass along this walkway every day to admire the paintings displayed in the walls.

38 39

Special features
There are eight pages that explore special kinds of buildings from the past and present. These pages compare ancient, modern, and religious buildings from around the world.

Equator

Stilt Hou...
Irian Jaya, Indon...

...ru
...s the highest
...ndonesian
...en of the 100
...still active.
...give off smoke
...y time. Although
...le live near
...h from volcanoes
...for farming.

Angkor Wat
Angkor Wat is a magnificent temple, built almost 900 years ago, which is hidden in Cambodia's steamy rain forest. It is the largest religious building in the world and contains many statues, courtyards, and galleries. Its unusual towers are built in the shape of lotus flower buds.

CAN YOU FIND...

❶ one of the large, thatched houses built by the Batak people? Up to 12 families live in one house.

❷ the world's widest waterfall? It stretches over 6 mi (10 km) across the Mekong River in Laos.

❸ flat fields, called te...ces, made by farmers to grow rice on hilly land...

❹ a statue of a merli... ...hich is a lionlike sea monster that has bec... ...he symbol of Singapore?

43

Can you find...
Can you match the description of each wonder with its picture? Each is numbered and matches up with a picture on the map.

Reading the maps
On each map, different colors and symbols show the types of land found around the world. Look below to see what these colors and symbols mean.

Rivers are large streams of water. Some swell to form lakes. Others travel down to the sea.

The land around the poles, in the far north and south of the world, is extremely cold and icy.

Grasslands are flat, dry areas covered with grasses and scattered with a few trees.

Evergreen forests stay green all year. They grow on mountains and in cold northern parts of the world.

Deciduous forests grow in cool parts of the world. The trees lose their leaves in winter.

Deserts are dry places where there is little rain. They can be hot or cold, rocky, or sandy.

Tropical rain forests are thick green forests that grow in hot, wet places near the equator.

Mountains are high rocky hills where the weather is windy and cold.

World map

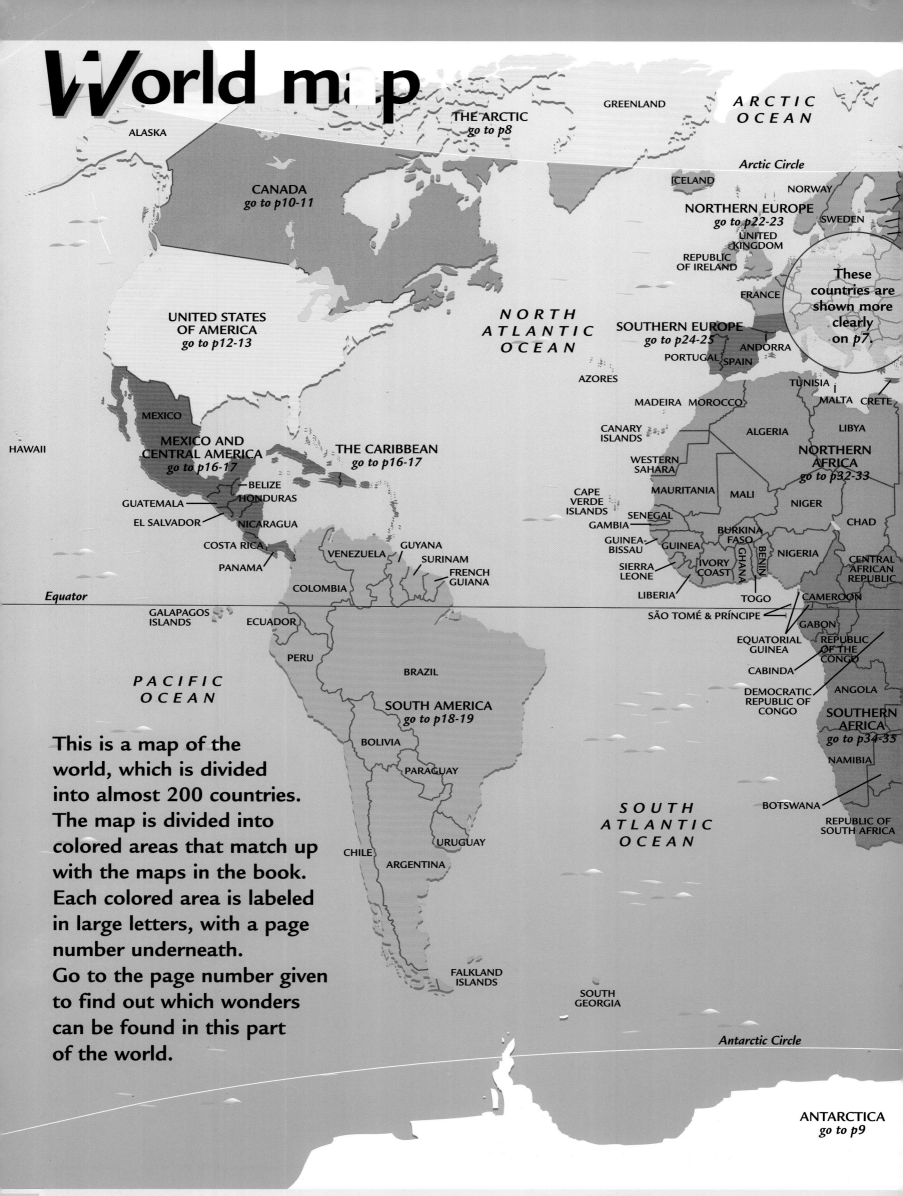

GREENLAND

THE ARCTIC
go to p8

ARCTIC OCEAN

ALASKA

Arctic Circle

ICELAND

NORWAY

CANADA
go to p10-11

NORTHERN EUROPE
go to p22-23

SWEDEN

UNITED KINGDOM

REPUBLIC OF IRELAND

These countries are shown more clearly on p7

UNITED STATES OF AMERICA
go to p12-13

NORTH ATLANTIC OCEAN

FRANCE

SOUTHERN EUROPE
go to p24-25

ANDORRA

PORTUGAL SPAIN

AZORES

TUNISIA

MALTA CRETE

MADEIRA MOROCCO

HAWAII

MEXICO

CANARY ISLANDS

ALGERIA

LIBYA

MEXICO AND CENTRAL AMERICA
go to p16-17

THE CARIBBEAN
go to p16-17

WESTERN SAHARA

NORTHERN AFRICA
go to p32-33

BELIZE

HONDURAS

CAPE VERDE ISLANDS

MAURITANIA

MALI

NIGER

GUATEMALA

EL SALVADOR

NICARAGUA

SENEGAL

GAMBIA

BURKINA FASO

CHAD

COSTA RICA

VENEZUELA

GUYANA

SURINAM

GUINEA-BISSAU

GUINEA

IVORY COAST

GHANA

BENIN

NIGERIA

PANAMA

FRENCH GUIANA

SIERRA LEONE

CENTRAL AFRICAN REPUBLIC

COLOMBIA

LIBERIA

TOGO

CAMEROON

SÃO TOMÉ & PRÍNCIPE

Equator

GALAPAGOS ISLANDS

ECUADOR

GABON

EQUATORIAL GUINEA

REPUBLIC OF THE CONGO

PACIFIC OCEAN

PERU

BRAZIL

CABINDA

DEMOCRATIC REPUBLIC OF CONGO

ANGOLA

SOUTH AMERICA
go to p18-19

BOLIVIA

SOUTHERN AFRICA
go to p34-35

This is a map of the world, which is divided into almost 200 countries. The map is divided into colored areas that match up with the maps in the book. Each colored area is labeled in large letters, with a page number underneath.
Go to the page number given to find out which wonders can be found in this part of the world.

PARAGUAY

NAMIBIA

SOUTH ATLANTIC OCEAN

BOTSWANA

URUGUAY

REPUBLIC OF SOUTH AFRICA

CHILE

ARGENTINA

FALKLAND ISLANDS

SOUTH GEORGIA

Antarctic Circle

ANTARCTICA
go to p9

THE ARCTIC
go to p8

RUSSIA AND ITS NEIGHBORS
go to p26-27

FINLAND
ESTONIA
LATVIA

KAZAKSTAN

MONGOLIA

UKRAINE
AZERBAIJAN
ARMENIA
GEORGIA
TURKEY
CYPRUS
SYRIA
LEBANON
IRAQ
JORDAN
ISRAEL
EGYPT
SAUDI
ARABIA

UZBEKISTAN
KYRGYZSTAN
TURKMENISTAN
TAJIKISTAN

EASTERN ASIA
go to p40-41

NORTH
KOREA
JAPAN
SOUTH
KOREA

PACIFIC
OCEAN

AFGHANISTAN

IRAN
KUWAIT
BAHRAIN
QATAR
UNITED
ARAB
EMIRATES

CHINA

BHUTAN

PAKISTAN

NEPAL

INDIA

SOUTHERN ASIA
go to p36-37

SOUTHWEST ASIA
go to p30-31

OMAN

MACAU

TAIWAN

MYANMAR

BANGLADESH

HONG
KONG

LAOS

VIETNAM

NORTHERN
MARIANAS

GUAM

SUDAN
ERITREA
YEMEN

DJIBOUTI

ETHIOPIA

SOCOTRA

THAILAND

ANDAMAN
ISLANDS

SOUTHEAST ASIA
go to p42-43

CAMBODIA

PHILIPPINES

PALAU

MARSHALL
ISLANDS

NICOBAR
ISLANDS

BRUNEI

UGANDA
SOMALIA

MALDIVE
ISLANDS

SRI
LANKA

MALAYSIA

STATES OF MICRONESIA

KENYA
RWANDA
BURUNDI

INDIAN
OCEAN

SINGAPORE

NAURU
KIRIBATI

TANZANIA

SEYCHELLES

INDONESIA

IRIAN JAYA

TUVALU

ZAMBIA
COMOROS
MALAWI
MAYOTTE

PAPUA NEW
GUINEA

SOLOMON
ISLANDS

ZIMBABWE
MADAGASCAR

THE PACIFIC
ISLANDS
go to p44-45

MOZAMBIQUE

VANUATU

FIJI

SWAZILAND

AUSTRALIA

NEW
CALEDONIA

LESOTHO

AUSTRALIA AND
NEW ZEALAND
go to p44-45

TASMANIA

NEW ZEALAND

SWEDEN
LATVIA
LITHUANIA
DENMARK
(Russia)
THE NETHERLANDS
BELARUS
GERMANY
POLAND
BELGIUM
LUXEMBOURG
CZECH
REPUBLIC
UKRAINE
LIECHTENSTEIN
SLOVAKIA
FRANCE
MOLDOVA
AUSTRIA
HUNGARY
SWITZERLAND
SLOVENIA
ROMANIA
MONACO
SAN
MARINO
CROATIA
FEDERAL
REPUBLIC OF
YUGOSLAVIA
BOSNIA
HERZEGOVINA
ITALY
BULGARIA
CORSICA
TURKEY
MACEDONIA
SARDINIA
ALBANIA
VATICAN
CITY
GREECE
SICILY

Many countries in Europe are
close together. In this circle, we
have made these countries bigger so
that you can see them more easily.

The Arctic

The Arctic is an ice-cold area at the far north of the Earth, made up mostly of ocean. In winter, the sun rarely shines, and much of the Arctic Ocean and the surrounding land, called **tundra**, freeze solid. In summer, some of the ice melts, and for a short time the tundra bursts into flower.

North Pole

The windswept North Pole is the most northern place on Earth. It lies in the middle of the Arctic Ocean and is frozen all year around. Modern explorers still travel the route of Robert Peary who, in 1909, was one of the first people to reach the North Pole.

Map labels

Mackenzie River (go to p10)

Trans-Alaska Pipeline

Northern Lights

Tundra (go to p10)

North Pole

Tents of the Nentsi People

Alert Station

Nordvest Fjord

Svalbard Islands

Arctic Circle

Snapfacts

*Nordvest Fjord is a narrow sea inlet that flows between steep cliffs. It is the longest **fjord** in the world.*

Svalbard is a group of icy islands whose name means "cold coast."

The Alert Station lies farther north than any other building on Earth. A few people live and work here.

CAN YOU FIND...

❶ the tough, movable homes of an Arctic people who herd reindeer and catch fish on the icy tundra, near the coast of northern Russia?

❷ a giant pipeline that carries oil all the way across Alaska? The oil is then loaded on tankers, which transport it to other parts of the United States.

Northern Lights

The Northern Lights, or Aurora Borealis, are flickering colored streaks and clouds that appear from time to time in the night sky. These dramatic displays can last for up to one hour, and people from all over the world gather to watch them.

Antarctica

Antarctica lies at the far south of the Earth. It is a mountainous, ice-covered **continent** that is windier than anywhere else in the world. Temperatures rarely reach above 32 °F (0 °C), which is colder than inside a freezer. A few buildings, used by scientists, dot the bleak landscape.

Amundsen-Scott Station

The Amundsen-Scott scientific station stands at the South Pole, which is the place farthest south on Earth. A shimmering dome protects the buildings and the scientists from the raging blizzards outside.

Map labels:
- N
- Transantarctic Mountains
- Lambert Glacier
- South Pole
- Ice Cave (2)
- Amundsen-Scott Station
- Ross Ice Shelf
- Mount Erebus (1)
- Iceberg
- Antarctic Circle

CAN YOU FIND...

1 Antarctica's most active volcano? Red-hot rock shoots out of its **crater** and crashes on the ice and snow below.

2 an enormous freezing cave hollowed out of a glacier? It changes shape constantly as water pounds at its sides, wearing the ice away.

Snapfacts

The Ross Ice Shelf is the largest raft of floating ice in the world. It is about as big as France!

The Transantarctic Mountains stretch thousands of miles across the entire continent of Antarctica.

*Lambert Glacier is the world's longest **glacier**. This huge river of ice moves slowly down to the coast.*

Iceberg

Giant chunks of ice, called icebergs, drift in the waters around Antarctica. They are molded into unusual shapes by the wind and waves. The largest iceberg ever seen was 60 mi. (100 km) wide and 180 mi. (300 km) long, which is about the same size as Belgium!

Canada

Much of this vast, rugged country is covered with dense pine forests, which are scattered with long, winding rivers, deep lakes, and plunging waterfalls. The Far North is an empty, frozen wasteland that borders the Arctic. But in the south, it is warmer and there are busy cities with spectacular modern buildings.

Rocky Mountains

The jagged Rocky Mountains stretch all the way down from Alaska, along the west coast of Canada, and into the United States. Every year, thousands of visitors climb the steep slopes. Here they can marvel at the bare mountain peaks and glimpse icy-blue lakes fringed with fir and pine trees.

Arctic Ocean

Yukon River

Mackenzie River

Great Bear Lake

Tundra

Rocky Mountains

Great Slave Lake

Nelson River

Totem Pole

Dinosaur Provincial Park

Trans-Canada Highway

Snapfacts

In winter, the **tundra** is freezing cold and deserted but in summer small plants grow. Animals visit the tundra to feed on these plants.

The Trans-Canada Highway is a road that stretches about 5,000 mi. (8,000 km), from the east to the west coast of Canada.

Lake Superior is the largest freshwater lake in the world.

Geodesic Dome

This unusual building in Montreal looks like a giant golf ball. It was built for the Expo 67 world's fair in 1967 and is made of thousands of see-through plastic panels, which are held together by steel tubes. Each panel is extremely light, so builders can join them together easily.

Niagara Falls

Niagara Falls lies on the border between Canada and the United States. Every day, millions of gallons of water plunge over a rocky ledge at the top of the falls. Down below, boats take visitors as close as they dare to the thundering water.

Arctic Circle

Hudson Bay

Turf Houses

4

Château Frontenac

St Lawrence River

3

CN Tower

Lake Superior

Geodesic Dome

Niagara Falls

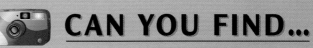

CAN YOU FIND...

1 a park named after the dinosaurs that roamed here 75 million years ago? Hundreds of dinosaur fossils have been found buried in rocks in the park.

2 a river that is the start of a network of rivers and canals, running from the Arctic Ocean to the Gulf of Mexico?

3 a building that looks like a French castle? It is in Quebec City, one of Canada's French-speaking cities.

4 houses with roofs covered in grass, called turf, to keep in the heat during bitter weather?

Totem Pole

This brightly painted totem pole stands in Stanley Park in Vancouver. It was carved by **Native Americans** from the trunk of a single cedar tree and shows fierce birds and other animals from ancient legends. In the past, a totem pole was often built into the entrance of a Native American chief's home as a sign of his power.

CN Tower

This needle-shaped communication tower rises up 1,815 ft. (553 m) into the clouds. It is the tallest **free-standing** building in the world and dominates the skyline above the city of Toronto. There is a section called the Sky Pod, which has viewing decks and a restaurant inside. The Sky Pod spins around slowly to give visitors a breathtaking view of the whole city below.

The United States

The United States is famous for its busy cities, such as Chicago and New York, which are packed with towering skyscrapers. There are also vast areas of land, called National Parks, which are protected for their beauty and wildlife. These parks range from scorching deserts and rugged mountains in the west to steamy swamps in the southeast.

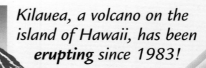

Trans-Alaska Pipeline (go to p8)

ALASKA

Rocky Mountains (go to p10)

Golden Gate Bridge

Colorado River

San Andreas Fault

Grand Canyon

Meteor Crater

Kilauea Volcano

HAWAII

Golden Gate Bridge
This 8,981-ft. (2.737-m) bridge spans the entrance to San Francisco Bay, linking the city of San Francisco with the rest of California. A giant six-lane road hangs from a pair of looping steel cables that run between two red towers.

Grand Canyon
For millions of years, the Colorado River has been carving away at the Grand Canyon in the Arizona desert. The river water has **eroded** the rocks, creating brightly colored layers. The river now flows along the cool and shady canyon floor.

Snapfacts

The San Andreas Fault is a 600-mi. (970-km) long crack in the Earth's surface. Many earthquakes begin here.

Many years ago, a huge object from space crashed in Arizona. It left a crater about a half mile (1 km) wide.

*Kilauea, a volcano on the island of Hawaii, has been **erupting** since 1983!*

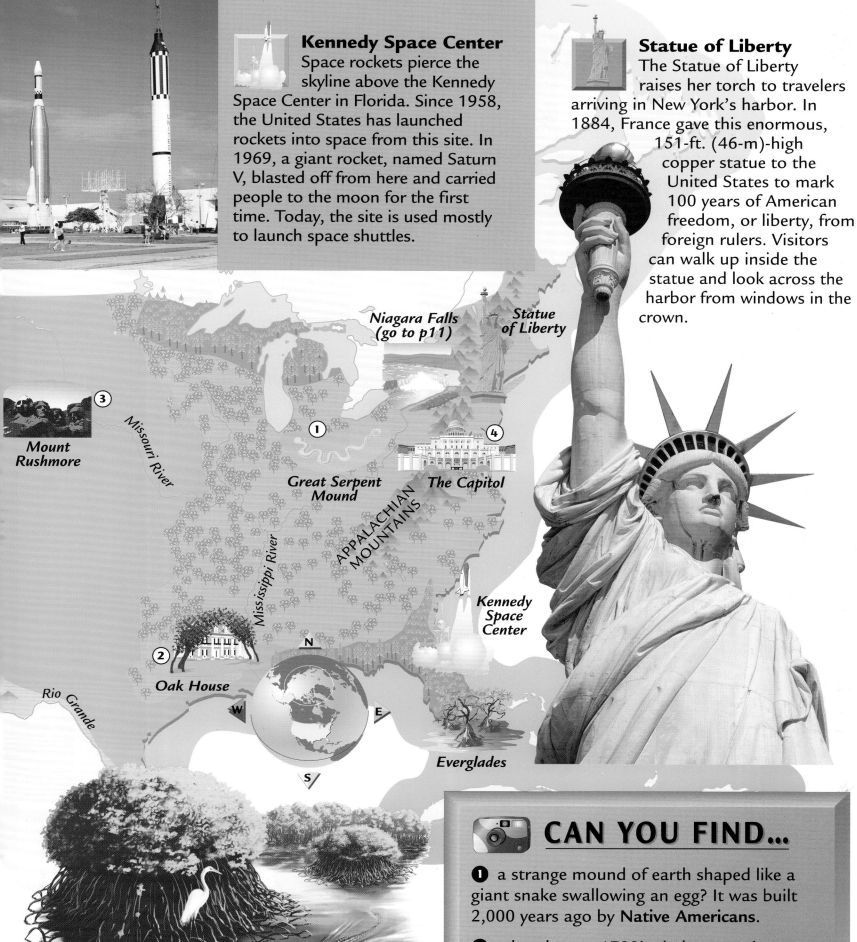

Kennedy Space Center
Space rockets pierce the skyline above the Kennedy Space Center in Florida. Since 1958, the United States has launched rockets into space from this site. In 1969, a giant rocket, named Saturn V, blasted off from here and carried people to the moon for the first time. Today, the site is used mostly to launch space shuttles.

Statue of Liberty
The Statue of Liberty raises her torch to travelers arriving in New York's harbor. In 1884, France gave this enormous, 151-ft. (46-m)-high copper statue to the United States to mark 100 years of American freedom, or liberty, from foreign rulers. Visitors can walk up inside the statue and look across the harbor from windows in the crown.

Niagara Falls
(go to p11)

Statue
of Liberty

Mount
Rushmore

Missouri River

①

④

Great Serpent
Mound

The Capitol

APPALACHIAN
MOUNTAINS

Mississippi River

Kennedy
Space
Center

②

Oak House

N

W   E

S

Rio Grande

Everglades

Everglades
These swamps and marshes in southern Florida are home to many rare animals and birds. Near the south coast, the long, crooked roots of mangrove trees arch into the mud, and alligators lurk in the murky waters, searching for food. Farther inland, the mangroves give way to tall grasses and freshwater animals.

📷 CAN YOU FIND...

❶ a strange mound of earth shaped like a giant snake swallowing an egg? It was built 2,000 years ago by **Native Americans**.

❷ a handsome, 1700's timber mansion at the end of a tree-lined avenue in Louisiana?

❸ the faces of four U.S. presidents carved into the side of a mountain? Each head is as high as a five-story building.

❹ a grand marble building in Washington D.C., where laws are made?

Ancient wonders

Over 2,000 years ago, around 100 B.C., a Greek writer listed the most beautiful sculptures, temples, **tombs,** and other structures that had ever been built. The top seven of these came to be known as the Seven Wonders of the Ancient World. Today, the only ancient wonder that still stands is the group of pyramids at Giza in Egypt.

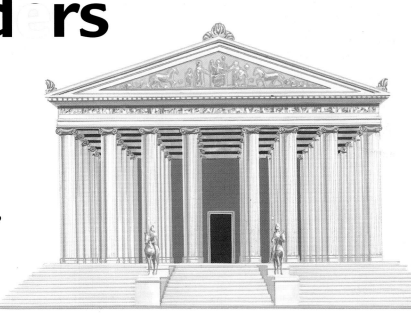

Temple of Artemis
This ancient temple, named after the goddess Artemis, stood in the Greek city of Ephesus until 356 B.C., when it burned down.

Statue of Zeus
Around 435 B.C., in Olympia, the ancient Greeks carved a huge ivory and gold statue of Zeus, their most important god.

Hanging Gardens of Babylon
These beautiful gardens contained hundreds of trees and flowers. They were built in Iraq around 605 B.C.

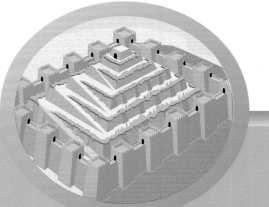

The Hanging Gardens of Babylon grew on a roof **terrace.** They were probably built by King Nebuchadnezzar II for his wife, who missed her old home in the mountains.

The Temple of Artemis was famous for its 106 magnificent, marble columns. They were all highly decorated. Today, **architects** still design buildings with these kinds of columns.

The Statue of Zeus held a small winged figure in his right hand. This was Nike who was the goddess of victory and the gods' messenger. Zeus carried a long scepter, or staff, in his left hand.

Pyramids
The Pyramids are the oldest of the Seven Wonders of the Ancient World. They were built around 2600 B.C. Egyptian kings were buried inside with many of their treasures.

Colossus of Rhodes
This impressive bronze statue looked out from the Greek island of Rhodes, until it fell to the ground during an earthquake in 224 B.C.

Mausoleum
The Mausoleum was a giant tomb in Turkey. Its name comes from the ruler, Mausolus, who was buried here around 353 B.C.

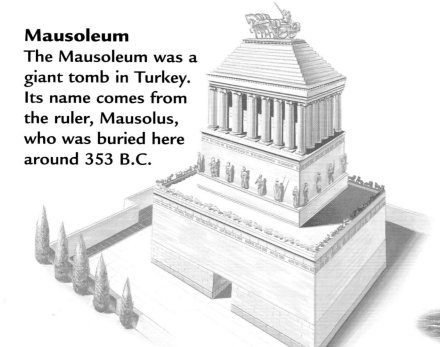

Lighthouse of Alexandria
This tall lighthouse, completed in about 270 B.C., stood in the harbor of Alexandria, in Egypt.

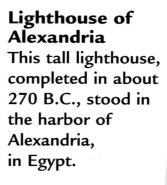

The Mausoleum was famous for its huge size and decoration. On top of the tomb, there was a large statue of Mausolus driving his chariot. A magnificent **frieze** ran along the base.

The Colossus of Rhodes was about 120 ft. (37 m) high, which is about as tall as the Statue of Liberty. The people of Rhodes built the statue to thank their god Helios for protecting them in battle.

For about 1,500 years, a fire burned at the top of the Lighthouse of Alexandria, guiding ships safely into the harbor. All the firewood had to be carried to the top by mule.

Mexico, Central America, and the Caribbean

Hidden high in the mountains and deep in the damp rain forests of Mexico and Central America, there are the remains of giant stone cities built thousands of years ago. The Caribbean Islands lie off the coast of Central America. In the past, they were home to the Carib Indians but now they are popular vacation spots.

Tula Columns, Mexico

Azteca Stadium, Mexico

El Castillo
Over 1,000 years ago, at Chichen Itza, a **Native American** people, called the Maya, built a flat-topped pyramid to honor their god, who was a feathered snake, called Kukulkan. The pyramid has 365 steps, one for each day of the year. Every March, huge crowds gather to watch the sun cast shadows on the staircase. The light plays tricks, making it look as if an enormous snake is slithering to the top.

Snapfacts

*Volcán Poas is a volcano that has left behind three **craters**. One is filled with cold water, one with hot water, and the third with trees.*

*The Arecibo **radio telescope** is the largest in the world. If 250 people held hands, they would still not stretch across its huge dish.*

Pitch Lake is a natural source of tar, which is used to build roads.

Tula Columns

These 16.5-ft. (5-m) stone statues were carved by an ancient people known as the Toltecs. The statues were used to hold up the roof of a temple in the city of Tula. The roof has long since collapsed, but the statues, showing the powerful warrior god Quetzalcoatl, still stand today.

Olmec Stone Head

About 3,000 years ago, the Olmecs were one of the first peoples to live in Mexico. They sculpted massive stone heads with serious faces that stood in the capital city, La Venta. Each head was a huge block of rock that was probably carried from a **quarry** over 60 mi. (100 km) away. The heads show the faces of Olmec rulers.

Island of Antigua

Antigua forms part of an arc of tropical islands that stretch across the Caribbean Sea. Antigua has over 360 sandy beaches, fringed with swaying palm trees. The sunny weather and beautiful landscape make it a popular vacation resort.

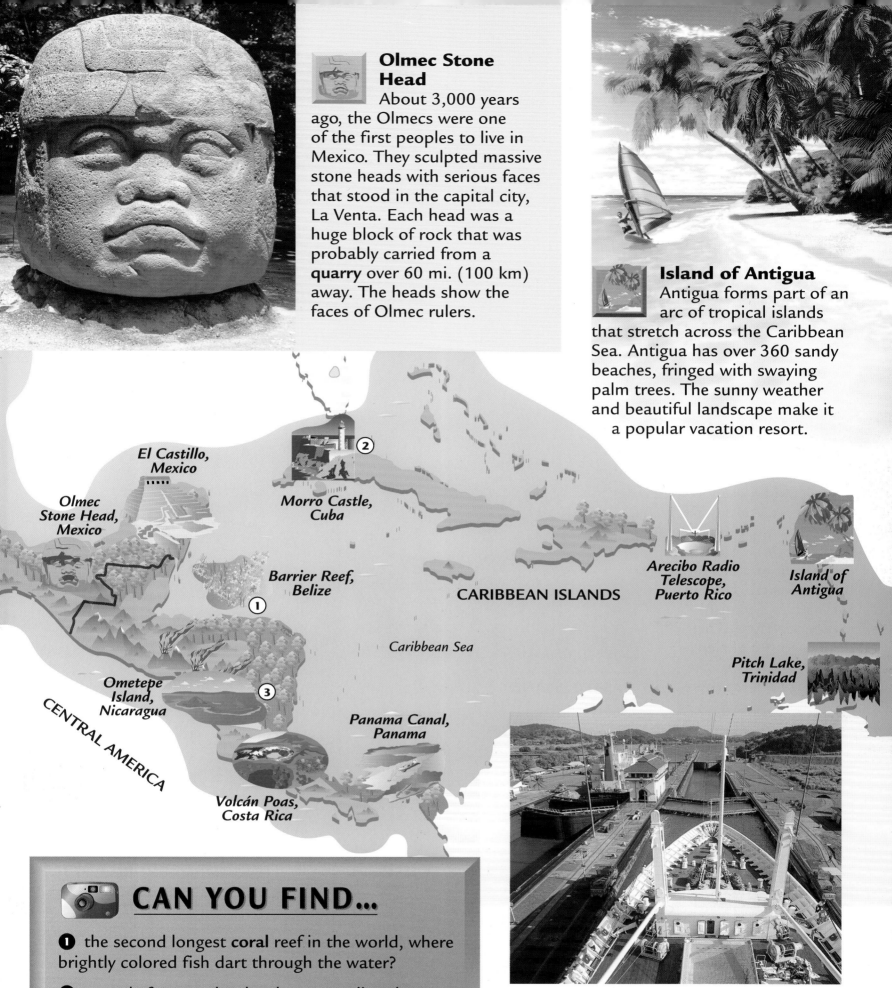

El Castillo, Mexico

Olmec Stone Head, Mexico

Morro Castle, Cuba

②

Barrier Reef, Belize

①

CARIBBEAN ISLANDS

Caribbean Sea

Arecibo Radio Telescope, Puerto Rico

Island of Antigua

Pitch Lake, Trinidad

Ometepe Island, Nicaragua

③

Panama Canal, Panama

CENTRAL AMERICA

Volcán Poas, Costa Rica

CAN YOU FIND...

❶ the second longest **coral** reef in the world, where brightly colored fish dart through the water?

❷ a castle fortress that has been guarding the entrance to Havana harbor since 1630?

❸ an island on the largest lake in Central America? There are two volcanoes here.

❹ an enormous **concrete** soccer stadium in Mexico City, one of the largest cities in the world?

Panama Canal

It took 30 years to build this vital short cut for ships sailing between the Atlantic and Pacific oceans. Before 1914, ships had to sail over 7,200 mi. (12,000 km) around the tip of South America. Today, they can sail along the canal, which extends 50.72 mi. (81.63 km).

South America

South America is a **continent** with amazing natural features, including the largest rain forest, longest mountain range, and highest waterfall in the world. It is a land of huge contrasts, with the remains of ancient towns and **civilizations** close to modern cities, where there are new, dramatic buildings.

Machu Picchu

In 1911, the Inca town of Machu Picchu was discovered high up in the Andes Mountains. Among the ruins, there was a royal palace and a temple. For centuries, the Incas lived in cities on the mountainside. Then in the 1500's, Spanish invaders arrived. They destroyed the ancient cities and many of the people who lived there.

Amazon Rain forest

This huge **tropical** rain forest lies along the banks of the meandering Amazon River. It covers most of Brazil and parts of many other countries. There are thousands of different kinds of trees that are home to animals, such as jaguars, snakes, and toucans.

Orinoco River

Angel Falls, Venezuela

Equator

Amazon Rain forest, Brazil

Amazon River, Brazil

São Francisco

Brasilia Cathedral, Brazil

Easter Island Statues, Chile

EASTER ISLAND

Machu Picchu, Peru

① Christ the Redeemer Statue, Brazil

Lake Titicaca, Peru/Bolivia

Itaipú Dam, Brazil/Paraguay

③

European Southern Observatory, Chile

Paraná River

④

Andes Mountains, Argentina/Chile/Peru

N

E

S

②

Torres del Paine, Chile

Snapfacts

The Amazon River is the world's second longest river. Its source was only discovered in 1971.

Lake Titicaca is one of the highest lakes in the world. People make boats from reeds that grow at the edge of the lake.

The Itaipú Dam, at the world's largest power plant, helps to power vast areas of Brazil and Paraguay.

Brasília Cathedral

This striking modern **cathedral** was built in 1960 in Brasília, the capital of Brazil. It is designed to look like the crown of thorns Jesus is said to have worn on the cross.

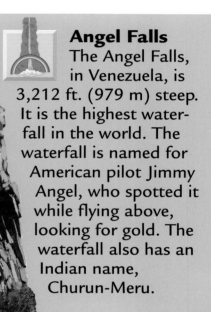

Angel Falls

The Angel Falls, in Venezuela, is 3,212 ft. (979 m) steep. It is the highest waterfall in the world. The waterfall is named for American pilot Jimmy Angel, who spotted it while flying above, looking for gold. The waterfall also has an Indian name, Churun-Meru.

Easter Island Statues

The small and volcanic Easter Island lies in the South Pacific Ocean. Polynesian people live here, along with over 600 large stone statues. The statues have big square faces and cast long shadows on the ground. No one is sure what the statues are for, but the early islanders must have worked in large groups to put them in place.

CAN YOU FIND...

❶ a huge statue called Christ the Redeemer, which stands atop Corcovado Mountain overlooking the city of Rio de Janeiro, in Brazil?

❷ spectacular pink granite and slate pinnacles among high mountain peaks at the southern tip of the Andes?

❸ a group of dome-shaped buildings on a mountaintop in Chile, from which **astronomers** study the stars?

❹ a long chain of mountains that stretches all the way down the coast of South America?

Castles

For centuries, kings, queens, and nobles protected themselves from enemy attack in strong, high-walled castles. But often castles were more than just **fortresses**. They were also homes, prisons, places where soldiers lived, and where treasure was stored. Throughout the world, all kinds of magnificent castles still stand today.

Alhambra

The Alhambra is a Spanish hilltop castle. It was built by a people called the Moors who ruled much of Spain from the 700's until the 1200's.

Windsor Castle

This large castle in the United Kingdom is still used as a home by Queen Elizabeth II.

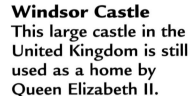

Krak des Chevaliers

This solid fortress in Syria was a stronghold for Christian soldiers who invaded the area in the 1100's.

Krak des Chevaliers is surrounded by two high, stone walls, which are separated by a steep slope. There was room for up to 2,000 soldiers, and stores of food that could last for up to five years.

Inside the Alhambra, there are elegant courtyards with beautifully carved marble decoration. Moorish princes relaxed here next to fragrant plants and bubbling fountains.

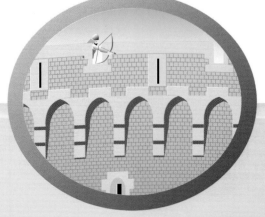

In the past, royal soldiers hid behind the **crenellations** at the top of the walls of Windsor Castle. From here, they threw heavy rocks and shot arrows at enemies below.

Azay-le-Rideau

French nobles made their home in this luxurious castle. It was built in the 1500's on an island near the River Loire.

Osaka Castle

Osaka Castle was built in 1584 for a powerful Japanese Samurai warrior.

Taourit Kasbah

North African mud castles are called kasbahs. This one in Morocco looks ancient, but it was built in the 1930's.

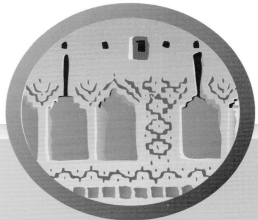

Azay-le-Rideau has a tall **turret** at each corner of the castle. Turrets helped to make early castles safe from attack. When this castle was built turrets were mostly added for decoration.

Fierce fish-tailed monsters perch on top of Osaka Castle. When it was built, people believed that these monsters would stop evil spirits from setting the wooden roofs on fire.

Taourit Kasbah is made entirely from mud. First, mud bricks were put into place to give the kasbah its shape. Then decorations were carved into the walls and left to bake dry in the hot sun.

North rn Europ

Northern Europe has a rugged coastline, dotted with islands. In the far north, where it is cold for most of the year, the landscape is dominated by mountains, pine forests, and lakes. In warmer areas farther south, there are flatlands with many towns. The mountains of the Alps separate this area from southern Europe.

Arctic Circle

③ Strokkur Geyser, Iceland

ICELAND

Borgund Stave Church, Norway

Great Glen, Scotland

② Kalmar Castle, Sweden

Giant's Causeway, Northern Ireland

Stonehenge, England

Elbe

① Brandenburg Gate, Germany

N
W E
S

Channel Tunnel, England/France

Windmills, Netherlands

Neuschwanstein Castle, Germany

Loire

Seine

Eiffel Tower, France (go to p24)

Iceman, Austria/Italy

ALPS

Danube

④ Parliament Building, Hungary

Stonehenge

These ancient stones, which once formed two circles, are over 3,500 years old. Some weigh as much as six elephants. Builders probably used wooden rollers and ropes to put them in place. No one knows why this mysterious monument was built, but it may have been used to follow the movements of the sun and moon.

Snapfacts

The Channel Tunnel, the world's longest undersea tunnel, measures nearly 31 mi. (50 km) total.

In 1991, a man's body was found in ice. The body, nicknamed Iceman, is thought to be over 5,000 years old.

The legendary Loch Ness monster is believed to live in a deep lake in the Great Glen valley.

Neuschwanstein Castle

This fairy-tale castle, with its high towers and **turrets**, was dreamed up by King Ludwig II of Bavaria. It sits on a rocky crag in the Alps. The building of the castle began in 1868, but Ludwig did not live long enough to see his dream come true.

CAN YOU FIND...

❶ a monumental stone gateway, built in 1791, that used to divide the city of Berlin? The gate has now become a symbol of peace.

❷ a medieval castle stronghold overlooking the sea? In 1397, the king of united Denmark, Norway, and Sweden was crowned here.

❸ a boiling fountain that shoots steam and water high into the air? This Icelandic geyser spouts every few minutes.

❹ a splendid building beside the Danube, where the Hungarian government meets?

Borgund Stave Church

Borgund Stave Church was built about 800 years ago. It is made entirely of wood with dramatic sloping roofs. On the doorways and the spires, there are intricate carvings of fabulous beasts from Viking legends.

Windmills

Many parts of the Netherlands lie below sea level. For hundreds of years, to fight against flooding, the Dutch have used windmills to drain water from the land. When the wind blows, a windmill's sails turn, powering a wheel that scoops water from the land into ditches and canals. Today, electric pumps do most of this work, but there are still many working windmills.

Giant's Causeway

These amazing rock columns look like giant stepping stones. Millions of years ago, **lava** was thrown out by volcanoes **erupting** nearby. The lava cooled slowly and steadily to form these regular six-sided pillars of solid **basalt**. There are about 40,000 columns altogether. Some are taller than a two-story house.

South rn Europ

Southern Europe lies along the northern shores of the Mediterranean Sea. Long, jagged mountain ranges, including the Alps and the Pyrenees, stretch across the land. Many historical cities here have magnificent remains from the ancient Roman Empire, which covered much of southern Europe around 2,000 years ago.

Eiffel Tower
This giant iron tower was designed by Gustave Eiffel as the entrance to the 1889 World's Fair in Paris. At the time, it was almost twice as high as any other building in the world. People called the tower the shame of Paris, but today it is one of the most famous buildings in Europe.

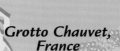

Eiffel Tower, France

Loire River

Grotto Chauvet, France

Po River

PYRENEES

Alps, France/Italy

Segovia Aqueduct, Spain

Sagrada Familia, Spain

Pena Palace, Portugal

Mediterranean Sea

📷 CAN YOU FIND...

❶ Europe's highest mountain range, which crosses seven countries? Its tallest peak, Mont Blanc, has a long tunnel through it, which connects France and Italy.

❷ a volcano on the Italian island of Sicily, which sometimes pours out ash and red-hot rock?

❸ the 4,000-year-old remains of a beautiful palace, which belonged to the king of Crete?

❹ a tall stone tower built in the 1100's as the bell tower for an Italian **cathedral**? Even before it was finished, the building began to lean to one side!

Sagrada Familia

This extraordinary church in Barcelona is still being finished, over 100 years after work began. It was designed by Antonio Gaudí, a Spanish **architect**. The outside is covered with thousands of sculptures that look like molded clay but are really made of stone.

Grotto Chauvet

Over 300 **prehistoric** paintings cover the walls of this hidden cave. The paintings were discovered in 1995, and many are believed to be over 32,000 years old. The pictures are mostly of animals, such as wild oxen, lions, and bears.

Danube

④ Leaning Tower of Pisa, Italy

Colosseum, Italy

Mount Etna, Sicily, Italy

②

Mediterranean Sea

Hagia Sophia, Turkey

Parthenon, Greece

③

Palace of Knossos, Crete, Greece

Snapfacts

Pena Palace was built in the 1800's for a prince. Its shocking pink and yellow walls make it look like a fairy-tale castle.

The huge, domed Hagia Sophia, was built over 1,400 years ago. It was first used as a church but today it is a museum.

This Roman aqueduct at Segovia carried water to nearby towns.

Colosseum

The Colosseum was built almost 2,000 years ago. It was the world's largest Roman **amphitheater**. Inside its **concrete**-covered walls, up to 50,000 people watched fierce contests between gladiators and wild animals, such as lions.

Parthenon

The Parthenon is an ancient temple that stands high on a hill called the Acropolis. It was built to honor the Greek goddess of wisdom, Athena. Today, only part of the Parthenon remains, but this picture shows you how it looked when it was first built.

Russia and its neighbors

Russia and its neighboring countries stretch across a vast area from eastern Europe to the tip of North America. For half of the year, much of the land is hidden by snow. In Russia, the largest country in the world, there are hundreds of beautiful religious buildings, and palaces built by the tsars who once ruled the country.

Taiga
Wolves and bears roam freely in the Russian taiga, which is the largest forest in the world. Taiga is a type of forest that grows where the winters are extremely cold. The trees are mainly evergreens, such as firs and pines.

Winter Palace, Russia
① Transfiguration Church, Russia
Arctic Circle
Ob Estuary, Russia
Space Obelisk, Russia
St. Basil's Cathedral, Russia
② Ural Mountains, Russia
Ob River
Don River
Volga River
Black Sea
Irtysh River
Caspian Sea
Aral Sea
Reghistan Square, Uzbekistan
Karakumsky Canal, Turkmenistan
③

St. Basil's Cathedral
This unusual, brightly painted **cathedral** overlooks the city of Moscow's famous Red Square. Each spectacular tower is topped by a colorful dome. The cathedral was built between 1555 and 1561 by the first czar of Russia, known as Ivan the Terrible.

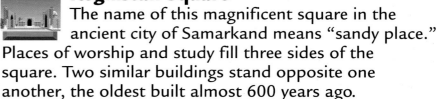

Reghistan Square
The name of this magnificent square in the ancient city of Samarkand means "sandy place." Places of worship and study fill three sides of the square. Two similar buildings stand opposite one another, the oldest built almost 600 years ago.

Snapfacts

The world's longest **estuary** stretches 531 mi. (885 km) from the Ob River to the Arctic Ocean. It is usually frozen for nine months of the year.

The Trans-Siberian Railroad is the longest railway in the world. It has 97 stops and is over 5,400 mi. (9,000 km) long.

Lake Baikal holds over one-fifth of the world's fresh water.

Frozen Mammoth Fossil, Russia

④

Yenisey River

Taiga, Russia

Lena

N

W   E

S

Amur

Trans-Siberian Railroad, Russia

Lake Baikal, Russia

Transfiguration Church

This church was built about 300 years ago on the island of Kizhi. It is made entirely of wood, but does not contain a single nail! Instead, wooden planks have been bent and slotted together. The church has 22 onion-shaped domes, each decorated with hundreds of tiny wooden tiles.

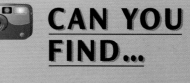

CAN YOU FIND...

❶ a palace in St. Petersburg that was the luxurious home of the Russian tsars? Today it is a museum and art gallery.

❷ a snowy mountain range that runs south from the **Arctic Circle**? The mountains separate Europe from Asia.

❸ a canal that carries water hundreds of miles to the dry desert of Turkmenistan so farmers can grow crops?

❹ the remains of a giant **prehistoric** elephant found in frozen ground in Siberia?

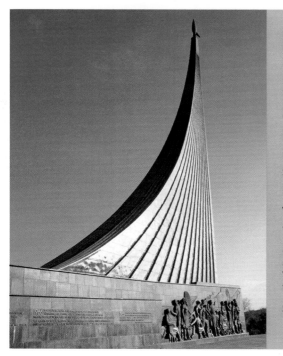

Space Obelisk

The Space Obelisk stands in a park in Moscow where the greatest achievements of the Russian people are remembered. It is a huge, steel monument, showing a rocket soaring into space above a thick wave of smoke. Russia was the first country to send an astronaut into space. The Space Obelisk celebrates this achievement and later successes in space.

Religious buildings

Across the world, there are millions of religious buildings, including churches, mosques, and synagogues, where people worship. Each building has its own kind of decoration, from soaring spires and minarets to huge domes and statues. Many of these buildings are on ancient sites that have a special meaning to followers of a religion.

Schwedagon Temple
Thousands of **stupas** make up this temple in Myanmar. The tallest one is covered in gold and jewels.

Canterbury Cathedral
Completed around 1070, Canterbury's handsome cathedral is the home of the Protestant Church of England.

St. Peter's Church
This Roman Catholic church, in Italy, is one of the largest in the world. It was built between 1506 and 1626.

From above, the main part of Canterbury Cathedral looks like a cross. This shape represents the cross on which followers believe that Jesus, the Son of God, died.

Thousands of Buddhists come to the Schwedagon Temple to leave offerings, such as lotus flowers. They believe that there are eight hairs belonging to the Buddha buried inside the temple.

Every Wednesday, the Pope, who is the head of the Roman Catholic Church, prays from the balcony of St. Peter's Church. Large crowds gather below, to listen to his words.

Royal Mosque at Esfahan

In 1612, building began on the Royal Mosque at Esfahan, in Iran. Today, Muslims from all over the world visit this mosque.

Beth Sholom Synagogue

The shape of this modern synagogue, in Elkins Park, Pennsylvania, was based on a mountain in Israel **sacred** to the Jewish people.

Meenakshi Temple

These colorful gateways, called gopurams, are part of a 1600's Hindu temple in southern India.

The entrance to the prayer hall of the Royal Mosque is covered in hand-painted tiles. Inside the hall, five times a day, Muslims kneel down on patterned rugs to pray to their god, Allah.

The Meenakshi Temple is covered with brightly painted plaster images of gods and goddesses. The temple honors the goddess Meenakshi and her husband Shiva.

Inside the Beth Shalom Synagogue, there is a light that shines above a chest containing God's Ten Commandments. This light is never allowed to go out.

Southwest Asia

More than 5,000 years ago, southwest Asia was home to many of the world's first **civilizations**. People settled near the great rivers in the north, away from the hot, dry desert farther south. Remains of their ancient cities can still be seen today. Several world religions began in southwest Asia, so there are also many **sacred** buildings here.

Hagia Sophia, Turkey (go to p25)

Urgup Cones, Turkey

Euphrates River, Turkey/Syria/Iraq

Pamukkale Springs, Turkey

Wailing Wall, Israel

Dead Sea, Israel/Jordan

Red Sea

Great Mosque and Kaaba, Saudi Arabia

Wailing Wall

The sound of sorrowful Jewish prayers gives the Wailing Wall its name. Jews gather at the foot of the wall to mourn the destruction of the Temple of Jerusalem. The temple was first built nearly 3,000 years ago. It was later destroyed and rebuilt several times. In 70 B.C., the Romans demolished the building for the last time. This massive stone wall is all that remains.

CAN YOU FIND...

❶ the ruins of an ancient city that burned down in 330 B.C.?

❷ a mountain where the Bible says Noah's Ark came to rest after the Great Flood?

❸ the longest river in southwest Asia, along which ancient civilizations grew up?

❹ an impressive tower with beautifully painted walls, still used today as a home?

❺ a large mosque that is covered inside and out with thousands of pale blue tiles?

Great Mosque and Kaaba

The Great Mosque in Mecca is the most sacred place in the world for Muslims, followers of the religion of Islam. In the courtyard of the mosque, there is a small, rectangular building called the Kaaba. This ancient **shrine** holds the Black Stone, which Muslims believe came from heaven. Every year, millions of Muslims worship at the Kaaba.

Pamukkale Springs

The Turkish name Pamukkale means "cotton castle," which is just what this sparkling white cliff looks like. For thousands of years, hot springs full of minerals have bubbled up from the ground, forming a series of "steps." People bathe in the pools of warm water. The minerals are thought to be good for the health.

Mount Ararat, Turkey

②

Imam Mosque, Iran

⑤

Salt Desert (Dasht-E Kavir)

N

W E

S

Barren Desert (Dasht-E Lut)

Ziggurat, Iraq

①

Persepolis, Iran

Great Sandy Desert (An Nafud)

Water Towers, Kuwait

Persian Gulf

Empty Quarter (Al Rub al Khali), Saudi Arabia

Tower House, Yemen

④

Snapfacts

The Ziggurat, or temple tower, in the ancient city of Ur was built about 4,000 years ago entirely from mud bricks.

The Dead Sea is nine times saltier than any ocean. The salt makes it easy for swimmers to float.

The Empty Quarter is one of the world's largest stretches of sand. It is so hot that few people come here.

Urgup Cones

These sand-colored cave homes, near the village of Urgup, are made of rock that **erupted** from volcanoes millions of years ago. The rock has been shaped into pointed cones by the wind and rain. More than 2,000 years ago, people widened holes and cracks in the rock to make homes. Today, many of the caves have been painted and become churches, but a few are still lived in by local farmers.

Water Towers

Kuwait lies in the desert and has no rivers. To make fresh water, salt is taken from seawater and the water is stored in tall towers. These needle-shaped towers hold over 2 million gallons (8 million liters) of water in two huge globes. One tower also has a restaurant and a garden. The third, thin tower lights up the others.

Northern Africa

More than half of northern Africa is covered by the baking hot Sahara. Few people live in the desert, but other parts of northern Africa have large cities with busy markets and beautiful mosques. The **fertile** Nile Valley runs down the east side of the desert. Thousands of years ago, the great kingdom of ancient Egypt grew up along the banks of this river.

Hassan II Mosque, Morocco

ATLAS MOUNTAINS

Paintings at Tassili n'Ajjer, Algeria

The Sahara, Mali/Algeria

AHAGGAR MOUNTAINS

Mopti Mosque, Mali

Niger

Lake Chad

③

Benin Bronzes, Nigeria

Lake Volta

Hassan II Mosque

King Hassan II of Morocco ordered this modern mosque, the tallest in the world, to be built in the city of Casablanca. It was completed in 1995. More than 25,000 worshipers can fit inside the prayer hall, where 50 glimmering crystal candelabras hang from the high ceiling. Part of the roof can slide back to convert the hall into an open-air area.

Snapfacts

The Nile is the longest river in the world. It starts as two rivers, the White Nile and the Blue Nile.

The Suez Canal, opened in 1869, allows ships to sail between the Red Sea and the Mediterranean Sea.

Paintings show that, thousands of years ago, cows grazed on the now barren land at Tassili n'Ajjer.

The Sahara

The Sahara is the largest desert in the world. Rolling sand dunes and rocky plains stretch from the Atlantic Ocean to the Red Sea. During the day, temperatures in the Sahara soar above 104 °F (40 °C), but at night they often plunge below freezing. Small fertile areas, called oases, lie throughout the Sahara. Here, people live in villages and grow crops.

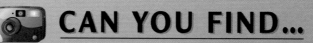

Mediterranean Sea

Great Sphinx, Egypt

Suez Canal, Egypt

Tutankhamen's Tomb, Egypt

Aswan High Dam, Egypt

❶

Nile River, Egypt

Red Sea

❹

Musgum Enclosure, Chad

❷

Churches of Lalibel, Ethiopia

N

W

E

S

Great Sphinx

This ancient stone monument has stood guard over the Egyptian pyramids at Giza for almost 4,500 years. The Sphinx was carved from a giant stone block in honor of Khafre, an Egyptian king who was buried in a **tomb** inside one of the pyramids. The Sphinx has a man's head and a lion's body. Its face has been partly worn away over the years by strong desert winds.

Mopti Mosque

The mosque at Mopti looks like an enormous sand castle. It was built in 1935 with mud bricks and wood. Every year, after the rainy season, the walls of the mosque have to be repaired and smoothed down by hand. A permanent wooden frame, built into the walls, makes it easy to carry out these repairs.

CAN YOU FIND...

❶ a massive **dam** built to hold back the waters of the Nile? It was opened in 1971 and, as well as controlling floods, it provides the area with electricity.

❷ a circle of cone-shaped, clay-covered huts that makes up a family farm?

❸ a group of beautiful bronze sculptures that are found at the site of an ancient kingdom?

❹ a group of churches carved from solid rock? The 11 churches were hacked out of hills and ditches about 800 years ago, during the reign of King Lalibel.

Tutankhamen's Tomb

In 1922, **archaeologists** discovered the tomb of Tutankhamen, an Egyptian king. Inside the tomb, there were thousands of priceless objects, such as golden bracelets and glistening thrones, that had not been touched for 3,000 years. One of the greatest treasures was a magnificent gold mask that covered Tutankhamen's head.

Southern Africa

Southern Africa is full of breathtaking natural wonders, including vast lakes, waterfalls, and valleys. Rivers wind through thick rain forests, and towering mountains rise above the African grassland, called savannah. Many different peoples live in southern Africa, some in traditional villages and others in busy, modern cities.

Zulu Village

More than 7 million Zulus make their home in South Africa. They traditionally live in round houses. These are made by covering a framework of hoops with matted reeds and thick layers of straw. The houses are arranged in circles to form small villages.

Mount Kilimanjaro

Africa's highest mountain is a **dormant** volcano. Giraffes feed on the grass and trees in the hot lands at the foot of the mountain. Its peak, 19,340 ft. (5,895 m) farther up, is so cold that it is covered in snow all year. On the mountain's lower slopes, farmers grow bananas, coffee, and corn.

Snapfacts

Lake Victoria is the largest lake in Africa and the second largest freshwater lake in the world.

*The great, winding Congo River flows for 2,900 mi. (4,667 km), crossing the **equator** twice.*

*The Okavango Delta is the largest inland **delta** on Earth. This wet wilderness is home to large flocks of birds and herds of hippos.*

Great Zimbabwe

For hundreds of years, the Shona people ruled part of Africa. They built a city called Great Zimbabwe, which became the center of their **empire**. Those who lived here were skilled miners and craftworkers. They mined gold, which they traded with overseas travelers. Today, the city's stone ruins include a circular granite wall that once enclosed many mud buildings.

Ndebele Houses

The Ndebele people of Zimbabwe and South Africa live in mud houses decorated with their own unique style of art. Ndebele women create the bold, colorful designs and then paint them on the outside walls of the houses, using brushes or their fingers.

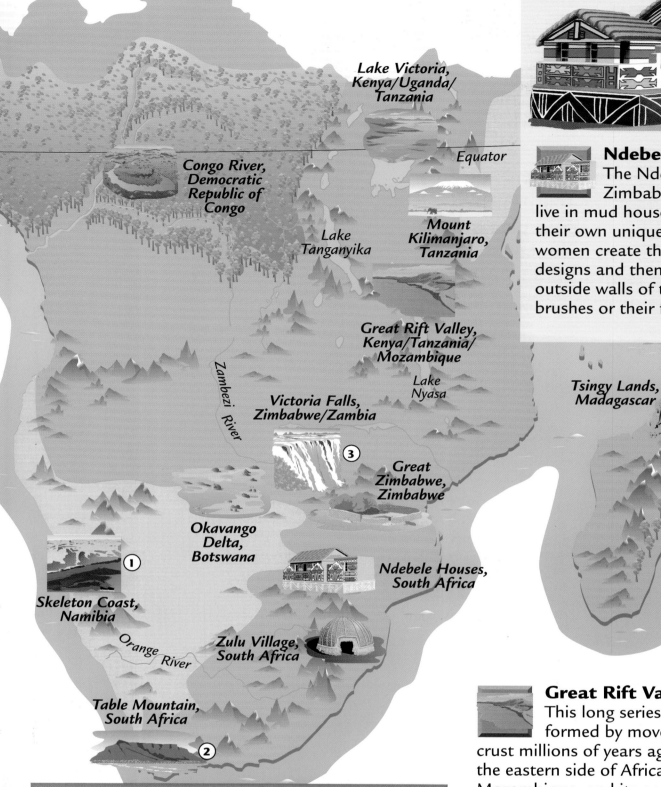

Lake Victoria, Kenya/Uganda/Tanzania

Congo River, Democratic Republic of Congo

Equator

Mount Kilimanjaro, Tanzania

Lake Tanganyika

Great Rift Valley, Kenya/Tanzania/Mozambique

Lake Nyasa

Zambezi River

Victoria Falls, Zimbabwe/Zambia

③

Great Zimbabwe, Zimbabwe

Okavango Delta, Botswana

Tsingy Lands, Madagascar ④

Ndebele Houses, South Africa

①

Skeleton Coast, Namibia

Orange River

Zulu Village, South Africa

Table Mountain, South Africa

②

N
W
E
S

CAN YOU FIND...

❶ a barren coast where the dry Namib Desert meets the sea? Its name comes from the many shipwrecks on its shores.

❷ a famous flat-topped mountain that overlooks a large city called Cape Town?

❸ a waterfall that creates so much spray that its mist can be seen from many miles away?

❹ a plateau full of razor-sharp, limestone spikes? It lies at the northern tip of Madagascar.

Great Rift Valley

This long series of deep valleys was formed by movements in the Earth's crust millions of years ago. It stretches down the eastern side of Africa, from Kenya to Mozambique, and its spectacular scenery includes lakes and volcanoes. In parts of the valley, fountains of steam and boiling water, called geysers, burst upward from the ground.

Southern Asia

Southern Asia stretches from the cold, snow-capped Himalaya in the north to the warm, green island of Sri Lanka in the south. Several different religions are practiced in southern Asia. Each religion has its own **sacred** places, including beautiful, ancient temples, where huge, colorful festivals are held and hundreds of people come to worship.

KARAKORAM RANGE

Helmand

Shah Faisal Mosque, Pakistan

③

Golden Temple, India

Indus

Taj Mahal, India

Thar Desert, Pakistan/India

②

Equator

Narmada

Godavari

Victoria Railroad Terminus, India

Nandi B India

①

Ganges River
The Ganges is one of the longest rivers in the world. Every year, up to 1 million people crowd its banks at the city of Varanasi and walk down the narrow steps to bathe in the water. Followers of the Hindu religion believe that the river is holy and that it will wash away their sins and cure their illnesses.

Maldive Islands

Taj Mahal
Many people think that the Taj Mahal, near the city of Agra, is one of the most beautiful buildings in the world. It is made of gleaming white marble and decorated with thousands of jewels. The Taj Mahal is a huge 1600's **tomb** built in memory of the wife of an Indian ruler named Shah Jahan. It took more than 20,000 people about 18 years to complete it.

Swayambhunath Stupa

This bell-shaped **stupa** is a holy monument of the Buddhist religion. Buddhists believe that the brightly colored flag streamers fluttering in the wind release hundreds of prayers into the world.

Snapfacts

The Maldives, in the Indian Ocean, is made up of 1,200 tiny **coral** islands. Most rise just 6 ft. (1.8 m) above the sea.

Victoria Terminus in Bombay is one of the world's busiest railway stations. It was built in 1887.

The Sundarbans is a swamp at the mouth of the Ganges, which is the world's biggest **delta**.

Himalaya, China/Nepal

Swayambhunath Stupa, Nepal

Brahmaputra

Ganges River, India/Bangladesh

Sundarbans, Bangladesh

Himalaya

The Himalaya, which divide western China from Nepal, India, and Bhutan, make up the world's highest mountain range. Its peaks are covered in ice and snow all year. Mount Everest, the highest mountain in the world, is part of this range.

Sigiriya Palace, Sri Lanka

Golden Temple

Every year, thousands of followers of the Sikh religion visit the Golden Temple in the city of Amritsar. This holy building sits on a platform in a sacred pool and shimmers in the water below. Its central dome and upper walls are covered with gold.

CAN YOU FIND...

❶ an enormous stone bull with a necklace of bells around its neck? A bull is an important symbol in the Hindu religion.

❷ a hot desert where an exciting festival is held? During the festival, people take part in camel races and play a ball game called polo.

❸ the largest mosque in the world? It was built in 1985 and is a mix of traditional and modern design.

❹ the remains of a magnificent palace, reached by climbing up a huge rock and passing between the paws of a stone lion?

Modern wonders

During the 1900's, new materials and modern technology have brought exciting advances in building design. Many cities are packed with towering skyscrapers and museums in unusual shapes. All of these places are built for the way we live today, and for how we plan to spend our time in the future.

Worker and the Collective Farm Girl.
This imposing steel statue was put up for an exhibition in Russia, in the 1940's.

Chrysler Building
The Chrysler Building was completed in 1930. It stands in New York, a city famous for its skyscrapers.

Guggenheim Museum
The Guggenheim Museum in New York City is made entirely out of **concrete**. Its smooth sides curve out and up, like a spring.

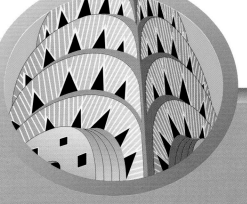

The Chrysler Building is an office built for a well-known car manufacturer. The gleaming metal circles at the top of the building were designed to look like giant car wheels.

The figures of the Worker and the Farm Girl carry a hammer and sickle in their hands. These tools of industry and farming are a symbol for how people can achieve more by working together.

Inside the Guggenheim Museum, a long spiral walkway curves all the way up to the roof. Hundreds of visitors pass along this walkway every day to admire the paintings displayed in the galleries.

Atomium
This unusual Belgian monument was built in 1958. It is made up of nine hollow balls, linked together by long metal tubes.

Pompidou Center
The unique design of the Pompidou Center, in France, shocked many people when it was built in the 1970's.

Petronas Towers
When these two 88-story office buildings in Malaysia were completed in 1996, they became the tallest in the world.

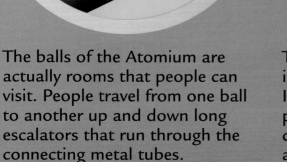

The balls of the Atomium are actually rooms that people can visit. People travel from one ball to another up and down long escalators that run through the connecting metal tubes.

The Pompidou Center looks like it has been turned inside out. Instead of having its everyday parts, such as escalators and air ducts, hidden on the inside, they are in full view on the outside.

The Petronas Towers are 1,483 ft. (452 m) high, nearly one and a half times higher than the Eiffel Tower in France. Two spires were added in a race to make the towers the tallest in the world.

Eastern Asia

Eastern Asia is a land of extremes with some of the world's driest deserts, highest mountains, and tallest office buildings. China is the biggest country in the area, stretching from the Himalaya in the west to the flat plains in the east. The Great Wall, the longest wall in the world, is found here.

Great Wall

The Great Wall of China is about 4,000 mi. (6,400 km) long, which is longer than the distance from London to New York. The wall snakes across the mountains of northern China. People started to build the wall over 2,000 years ago to defend China from attacks by northern invaders.

Forbidden City

The Forbidden City is in Beijing, the capital of China. A huge portrait of Mao Zedong, a famous Chinese leader, sits above the southern entrance. Inside the city, there is the Imperial Palace where Chinese emperors used to live.

Snapfacts

The Potala Palace, enlarged many times since it was first built during the 600's, has over 1,000 rooms.

At ice festivals in China, beautiful palaces and statues are cut out of vast blocks of ice.

Streams that flow into the Taklimakan Desert evaporate in the heat before reaching the sea.

Taklimakan Desert, China

HIMALAYA

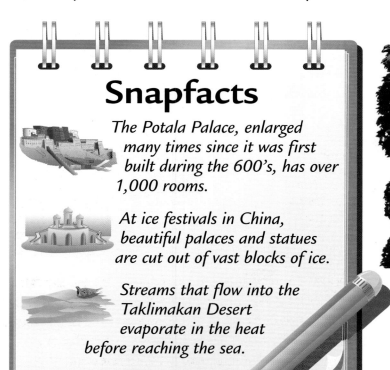

Flower Pagoda
Buddhist pagodas are religious buildings that have narrow towers and many roofs. This eight-sided pagoda was built 900 years ago and is called Huata or Flower Pagoda. Although it has nine roofs, the pagoda has 17 different floors inside it.

Mount Fuji

Mount Fuji is a volcano that last erupted in 1707. It has the highest peak in Japan, and its white top is often hidden by clouds. For many Japanese people the volcano is **sacred**. More than 50,000 people climb it every year.

CAN YOU FIND...

1 a tall brick tower, called a minaret, that is part of a simple, sand-colored mosque?

2 huge, high plains covering much of Mongolia? Traveling people who live here keep animals and sleep in tents called yurts.

3 a forest of needle-shaped rocks, **eroded** over thousands of years by wind and water?

4 a large bronze statue of Buddha, which has survived massive storms, earthquakes, and tidal waves since it was built in 1252?

Ice Palace, China

Great Buddha, Japan **4**

2 Mongolian Plains, Mongolia

Emin Minaret, China **1**

Forbidden City, China

Mount Fuji, Japan

Yellow River

Great Wall, China

Potala Palace, Tibet, China

Yangtze

3

Stone Forest, China

Flower Pagoda, China

Hong Kong and Shanghai Bank, Hong Kong

N

W   E

S

Hong Kong and Shanghai Bank

The towering Hong Kong and Shanghai Bank headquarters were built to squeeze as many offices as possible into a small area. Following old beliefs, experts advised on the best site for the building and which way it should face to bring good luck.

Southeast Asia

Southeast Asia is made up of a narrow strip of land and thousands of scattered islands. The area has hot, **tropical** forests, high mountains, and smoking volcanoes. There are more volcanic **eruptions** here than anywhere else in the world. In the cities, ancient religious monuments stand alongside spectacular modern skyscrapers.

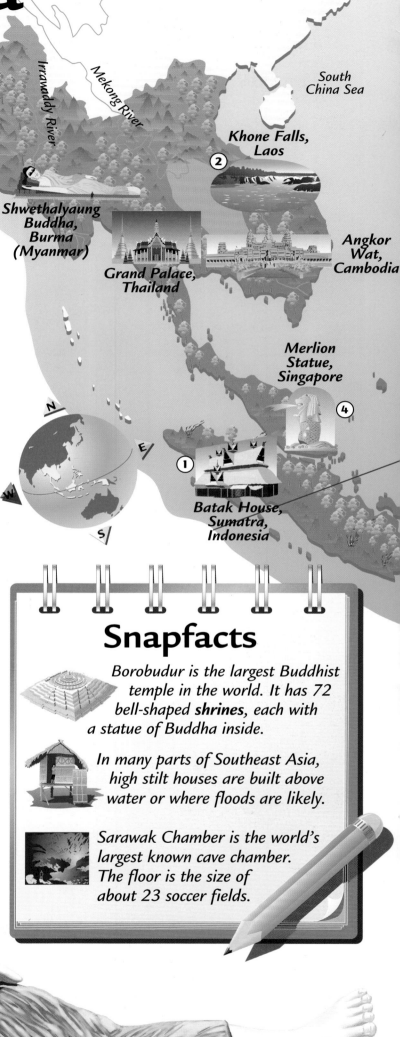

Irrawaddy River

Mekong River

South China Sea

Khone Falls, Laos

②

Shwethalyaung Buddha, Burma (Myanmar)

Grand Palace, Thailand

Angkor Wat, Cambodia

Merlion Statue, Singapore

④

①

Batak House, Sumatra, Indonesia

Grand Palace
The Grand Palace is a group of beautiful buildings in Thailand's bustling capital, Bangkok. A Thai king always spends his first night as king here. Orange-robed Buddhist monks come to worship at temples that lie inside the Grand Palace.

Shwethalyaung Buddha
This enormous, reclining statue of Buddha was built more than 1,000 years ago and is 30 times larger than life. The Buddha was left hidden 200 years ago, when the town of Bago was destroyed, and was only rediscovered in 1881 by a worker helping to clear the jungle.

Snapfacts

Borobudur is the largest Buddhist temple in the world. It has 72 bell-shaped **shrines**, each with a statue of Buddha inside.

In many parts of Southeast Asia, high stilt houses are built above water or where floods are likely.

Sarawak Chamber is the world's largest known cave chamber. The floor is the size of about 23 soccer fields.

Omar Ali Saifuddin Mosque

This mosque, named after the 28th Sultan of Brunei, was built in 1958. The gleaming gold and white mosque was designed in Malaysia, but the materials used in the building come from all over the world. The floors and walls are made of Italian marble and the stained-glass windows were crafted in England.

Rice Terraces, Philippines

③

Omar Ali Saifuddin Mosque, Brunei

Equator

Stilt Houses, Irian Jaya, Indonesia

Sarawak Chamber, Malaysia

Mount Semeru, Java, Indonesia

Borobudur, Java, Indonesia

Mount Semeru

This volcano is the highest peak on the Indonesian island of Java. Seventeen of the 100 volcanoes on Java are still active. This means that they give off smoke and could erupt at any time. Although it is dangerous, people live near volcanoes because ash from volcanoes makes the soil good for farming.

Angkor Wat

Angkor Wat is a magnificent temple, built almost 900 years ago, which is hidden in Cambodia's steamy rain forest. It is the largest religious building in the world and contains many statues, courtyards, and galleries. Its unusual towers are built in the shape of lotus flower buds.

CAN YOU FIND...

❶ one of the large, thatched houses built by the Batak people? Up to 12 families live in one house.

❷ the world's widest waterfall? It stretches over 6 mi. (10 km) across the Mekong River in Laos.

❸ flat fields, called **terraces**, made by farmers to grow rice on hilly land?

❹ a statue of a merlion, which is a lionlike sea monster that has become the symbol of Singapore?

Australia, New Zealand, and the Pacific Islands

Australia, New Zealand, and the Pacific Islands lie at the far south of the Earth. Australia is a hot **continent** famous for its dry grasslands and desert, known as the outback, and the carvings and paintings of a native people, called the Aborigines. The two islands that make up New Zealand are cooler with rich farmland and rocky mountains. Thousands of other smaller islands dot the Pacific Ocean.

Ayers Rock
Ayers Rock (called Uluru in Aboriginal) is a giant, sandstone rock that rises 1,142 ft. (348 m), dominating the flat desert landscape around it. At sunset, it glows bright red. It is **sacred** to the Aborigine people.

Lightning Brothers Rock Painting

④

Ayers Rock (Uluru)

AUSTRALIA

Lake Eyre

Great Victoria Desert

Coober Pedy

①

Wave Rock

Snapfacts

Lake Eyre is the largest lake in Australia. Most of the time, it is just dry mud, with a crust of salt about 13 ft. (4 m) thick!

In villages in Papua New Guinea, local people build special houses, where carvings of spirits are stored. These are called spirit houses.

Half of the world's opals come from the 100-year-old Coober Pedy mines.

Sydney Opera House
The roof of this world-famous building in Sydney Harbour looks like rows of giant sails. It is covered with more than 1 million white tiles that make it glint in the sunlight. Inside the building, there are four main halls for operas and concerts, 60 dressing rooms, and three restaurants. The Opera House took 14 years to build. It was opened in 1973.